CARD GAMES AND TRICKS

KU-711-921

A step-by-step guide to the world's greatest card games and tricks for adults or children

p

This is a Parragon Book
This edition published in 2004

Parragon
Queen Street House
4 Queen Street
Bath BA1 1HE. UK

Copyright © Parragon 1996

ISBN 1-40543-920-3

Printed in China

Contents

Start Here

Welcome to the colourful and exciting world of card games! In this book you will find clear explanations of thirty-five games, giving you the essential know-how for many more. Card games tend to come in 'families' with lots of variations. Once you know the basic game, it's easy to play the others. There are games here for you to play on your own, with one other person, or with three or more. In each section the games gradually become more complex.

THE BASICS

A standard pack of cards has 52 cards, divided into 4 suits of 13 cards each. The suits are clearly marked by their symbols – hearts, clubs, diamonds and spades. Each card has a value. Ace is either top or bottom, depending on the game. Then, from the top, king, queen, jack, and the number cards from 10 to 2. There is an extra card, not used in all games, the joker. He normally beats everything.

At the start of almost every game, the pack is shuffled, so that the cards are thoroughly mixed, and then cut. This means that a player other than the one who shuffled lifts around half of the shuffled stack and swaps the two halves around, so that the upper half becomes the lower half.

Card games are international, but beware – often there are differences between the British and the American versions of a game with the same name. Some games with the same name are quite different in the two countries. Even within a single country, there can be variations of the same game. It doesn't really matter. Just make sure that anyone you play with is playing to the same rules as you.

Most card games can be used for gambling, and some are designed for it. Currency can be anything from plastic tokens to the real thing – whatever it is, don't bet beyond your ability to pay.

Note of Apology:

In this book, players are referred to as 'he'. This is used as an abbreviation of 'he or she' and is not in any way meant to exclude female players from the pleasure of card-playing. Also, Bridge is not included here because the rules and methods of play would fill a short book like this many times over.

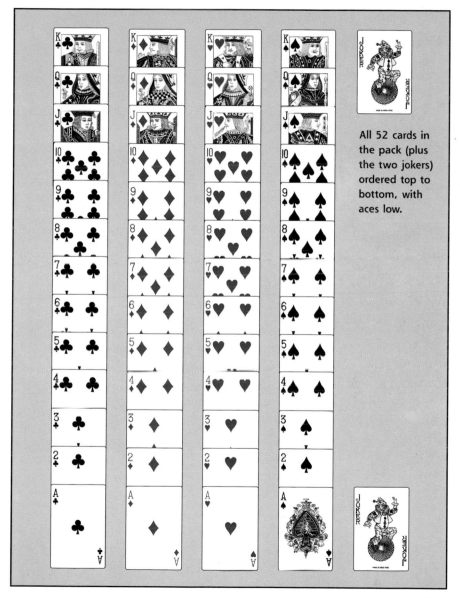

All 52 cards in the pack (plus the two jokers) ordered top to bottom, with aces low.

Technical Terms

Ace High: Ace is top scoring card (and Ace Low is the opposite).

Ante: The amount each player pays into the Pool at the beginning of a gambling game.

Available Card: In Patience, a card that can be used in play (depending upon the rules of the game).

Building Up: In Patience, laying cards in ascending order of value on top of a Foundation Card. Building Down is laying them in descending order.

Chips: Tokens used in gambling games; different chips can be given different values.

Column: Cards laid on the table in a vertical line (top of one meets or overlaps bottom of another).

Court Cards: Kings, queens and jacks.

Deal: Pass out cards to players. The dealer holds the pack face down, takes from the top, and goes clockwise around the players. Most deals are one card at a time to each player, but this can vary.

Deck: Another word applied to the Pack.

Discard: In some games, this means playing a card of no value in the game, when the player cannot Follow Suit or play a Trump; in others, it means playing a card to the Waste Pile.

File: In Patience, a column in the Layout, with cards overlapping, but with their suits and Pip Values visible. Files are built up towards the player.

Flush: A Hand of cards all of the same suit.

Follow Suit: To play a card of the same suit as the first card played in a Trick.

Foundation Card: In Patience, a card laid down on which other cards are built up or down. They are normally aces or kings.

Hand: The cards held by a player during the game. In Patience, it can also be any cards which have not been dealt out (also known as the Stock).

Honours: Ace, king, queen and jack of the Trump suit.

Layout: The arrangement of cards in Patience games. Also called the Tableau.

Lead: To play first to a Trick. Also the card played first (Lead Card).

Meld: A set of three or more of a kind, e.g. either all kings, or all hearts (but these must be in sequence of Pip Value with no gaps).

Pack: The full set of 52 cards (or 53 when the joker is included).

Packet: Part of a Pack.

Pair: Two cards of the same kind, e.g. two sevens.

Pass: To miss a turn.

Pip Value: The number of pips on a number card (e.g. a nine has nine pips).

Pool: The cash or gambling Chips staked in a game, usually placed in the middle of the table. Also called the 'kitty' or the 'pot'.

Plain Card: Card not of the Trump suit.

Play: To play a card is to take it from your hand and use it in the game.

Rank: The value of a card.

Redeal: In Patience, using the cards from the Waste Pile to deal again, when the Stock is used up.

Renege: To fail to follow suit in a game where following suit is not obligatory. Often confused with Revoke.

Revoke: To play an incorrect card, normally by failing to follow suit when able to, in a game when following suit is obligatory if you can do so. Often confused with Renege.

Round: This is complete when each player has played his cards in any Trick.

Row: In Patience, a line of cards placed side by side (suit and Pip Value must always be visible if the cards overlap).

Rubber: A set of games, especially in Whist and Bridge.

School: A group of players playing for money.

Sequence: The order in which the cards run, from high to low, or the other way round.

Singleton: A single card of any suit.

Stock: The cards remaining after dealing, sometimes also called the Hand.

Tableau: Another word for the Layout.

Talon: Another word for Waste Pile.

Trick: The cards played by all the players in a round, one from each. It is normally won, or taken, by the player who played the highest card in the leading suit, or the highest Trump.

Trumps: Cards of a chosen suit that outrank all cards in other suits during the game. Trumping (sometimes referred to as Ruffing in Whist and Bridge) is playing a Trump Card.

Waste Pile: Cards turned up in the course of playing Patience that are not available for play according to the rules of the game. Also sometimes referred to as the Talon.

Wild Card: A card which a player can use to represent any other card (within the rules of the game).

9

Clock Patience

AIM OF THE GAME: To arrange all of the cards in a clock-face formation, with the kings in the centre.

HOW TO PLAY: Use the standard 52-card pack. Deal out 13 packets of four cards, face down. Place 12 of the packets in a circular formation, like the numbers on a clock face. Place the 13th packet in the centre of the 'clock' to form the stock pile. Turn the top card of the stock pile face up.

If it is a queen, it counts as 12; if a jack, as 11; if an ace, as one. Other cards have numbers corresponding to their pip values, and your aim is to have them all at the right place on the 'clock': e.g. all four sixes at six o'clock and all queens at twelve o'clock.

Place the turned-up card in the right place on the clock face, under the packet, face up; turn over the top card of that packet. Place that card in its right place in the same manner; turn over the top card of that packet, and so on.

If you turn over a king, place him face up at the bottom of the stock pile, and turn over the top card on the stock pile.

Continue until all four kings have been turned up and placed in the stock pile. You win if the last card to be turned up is the fourth king, because by then you will have completed the clock.

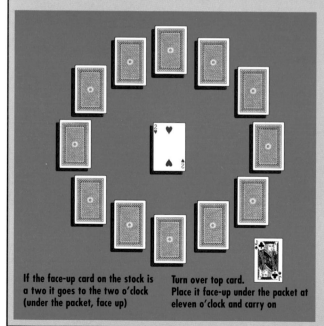

If the face-up card on the stock is a two it goes to the two o'clock (under the packet, face up)

Turn over top card. Place it face-up under the packet at eleven o'clock and carry on

Beggar Your Neighbour

AIM OF THE GAME: To win all 52 cards.

HOW TO PLAY: Use the standard pack of 52 cards. Cut for dealer (higher card). The non-dealer shuffles the cards. Each receives 26 cards.

The cards should be set out in a pile, face down. Each player turns over the top card and places it in front of his pile. The higher card wins the other (aces are low), and the player takes both cards and puts them face down. If two cards of the same value are turned over, then a 'war' is declared. The two equal cards are placed in the centre of the table. Each player makes a pile of three cards placed face down, with a fourth on top, face up. The higher of the face-up cards wins both piles, plus the two cards in the centre. If the two face-up cards are of equal value, the war is repeated, and the winner takes all the cards played. The game goes on until one player has all the cards.

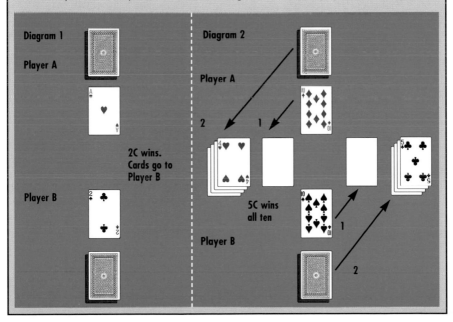

Old Maid

AIM OF THE GAME: To avoid being left holding the last queen.

NUMBER OF PLAYERS: Minimum of two, though many more can play.

HOW TO PLAY: Cut for dealer (higher card). Set aside the queen of clubs from a 52-card pack, and deal out the remaining 51 cards (one player will have an extra card).

Each player's cards are spread out, face up, and any pairs are removed and placed face up in the centre of the table. The rest of each hand is then shuffled, and the player holding the unpaired queen holds his hand up, cards hidden, for the opponent to draw a card from. If the drawn card makes a pair, the pair is discarded. It is then the opponent's turn to shuffle and offer the cards. Eventually, all the cards will be paired except for the one remaining queen – the old maid – and whoever is left with it loses the round. Play can go on for an agreed number of rounds, with the winner taking the most rounds.

Pelmanism (or Memory)

AIM OF THE GAME: To collect all, or most, of the cards.

NUMBER OF PLAYERS: Up to six can play, but two is best.

HOW TO PLAY: Cut the cards to determine who goes first (higher card). Spread out the entire pack (52 cards) face down, leaving space between each card.

The first player turns over any two cards. If they make a pair (same number or rank), he takes them out and stacks them in front of him. He then turns over two more, until he fails to make a pair. The cards that do not make a pair are returned face down to their original position, and the turn passes to the other player. The game continues until all the cards have been picked up: the player with the greatest number of tricks (pairs) is the winner.

HELPFUL HINT: A geographical memory is needed to win this game – try to remember the positions of the cards which have been turned up and then turned face down again.

German Whist

This is the best form of Whist for two players.

AIM OF THE GAME: To build a winning hand and score 50 points.

HOW TO PLAY: Use the 52-card pack. Cut for dealer (higher card). Dealer then deals 13 cards alternately to each player. The 27th card is turned over to denote trumps. The remainder forms the stock, face down.

The dealer leads a card, and the opponent can either beat it with a higher card of the same suit, or any trump (if trumps were not played), or he can play a lower card and lose the trick.

The winner of the first trick takes the face-up trump card, waits for his opponent to draw a fresh card from the stock, then turns over the next card.

The game continues until all the stock has been played: this marks the end of the first stage.

In the second stage, the players' hands are played out, with the winner of the last trick of the first stage taking the lead.

HELPFUL HINT: In the first stage of the game, it is vital to build up a strong hand in anticipation of the second stage.

SCORING: One point per trick. Target score is normally 50, although this can be varied by agreement among the players.

Your hand

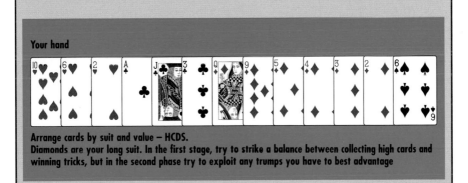

Arrange cards by suit and value – HCDS.
Diamonds are your long suit. In the first stage, try to strike a balance between collecting high cards and winning tricks, but in the second phase try to exploit any trumps you have to best advantage

Seven-Up

This game used to be known in Britain as All-Fours.

AIM OF THE GAME: To be first to reach seven points, by building up a trick-winning hand.

HOW TO PLAY: Use a 52-card pack. Draw for dealer – the higher card wins. Dealer deals six cards to each player, in two sets of three. The top card of the stock is then turned over to determine trumps. If a jack is turned up, the dealer gets one point.

The other player begins, by either standing (accepting the turned-up card as trumps) or begging (requesting a different suit). The dealer can accept or deny this request. If he accepts it, he deals three new cards to each and turns over the new top card of the stock, until a trump is agreed. If the dealer refuses to change trumps, the other player scores one point, and play continues.

Each player, if necessary, discards enough of his cards to reduce his hand to six. The non-dealer leads, placing a card face up. The dealer must follow suit, with a higher value, or play a trump to win the trick. Otherwise the trick is awarded to the other player. The winner of the trick leads the next card.

SCORING: Single points are won as follows:

HIGH: The player dealt the highest trump in play.

LOW: The player dealt the lowest trump in play.

JACK: The player winning the jack of trumps in a trick (unless the dealer turned it over to determine trumps).

GAME: The player with the highest total of point values for cards won in tricks. Values are: ace, 4; king, 3, queen, 2, jack, 1, ten, 10. No other cards have any value. If only one trump card is played, it collects two points, or three if it is the jack.

Stock

Trump

Your hand

1

Advice: Stand

Your hand

2

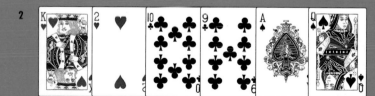

Advice: Beg

15

Gin Rummy

This is one of the many variations of Rummy.

AIM OF THE GAME: To build up a winning hand of melds (see Technical Terms page 8) and be first to score 100 points.

HOW TO PLAY: Cut for dealer, using the standard 52-card pack (aces high). Dealer shuffles, and deals ten cards to each player. The remaining cards, face down, form the stock. The top card is turned face up and placed by itself, to start the discard pile.

The other player has the option of taking that card or refusing it; he cannot draw a card from the stock pile. If he refuses it, the turn passes to the dealer. If the dealer also passes (refuses the turned-up card), the other player may take the top (face-down) card from stock. When a card is picked up, another must be placed on the discard pile.

The aim is to be the first to lay down all your cards in melds (sets of three or more cards of the same suit in consecutive numbers, counting from ace as low; or sets of three or more from different suits, but the same value).

If you have a full hand of melds, call out 'Gin!' You receive a bonus of 25 points plus the value of your opponent's unmelded cards. You can also choose to go out if you have some melds and the unmelded cards in your hand have a value of ten points or less, but if this is the case, then be careful because your opponent has the chance to complete his melds using your unmelded cards before the score is counted.

The player with the lower value of unmelded cards is awarded a bonus of 25 points.

If neither player has gone out before the last two cards are drawn from the stock, the round is treated as a no-score draw.

SCORING: Court cards (king, queen, jack): ten points each.
Ace: one point.
Number cards: as indicated by their pip value.
The value of the unmatched or unmelded cards still in your hand counts against you.
If the player who went out has the same, or greater, value of remaining cards as his opponent, the opponent receives a bonus of ten points together with the difference between the card values.
The winner of the game is the first player to reach 100 points.

Sample melds

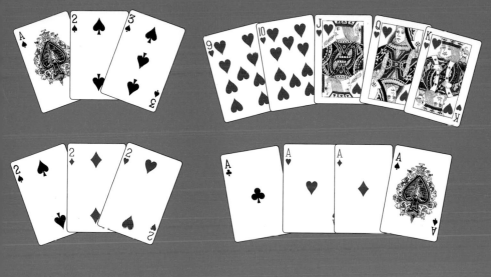

A dream hand

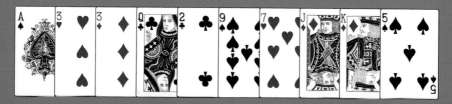

A hand from hell – no melds at all

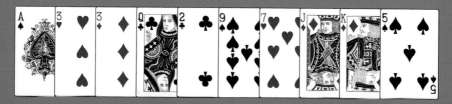

17

Sevens

AIM OF THE GAME: To get rid of all your cards.

NUMBER OF PLAYERS: Three to eight.

HOW TO PLAY: This is a gambling game, so each player starts off with an equal number of chips, and puts a chip into the pool at the start.

Use the pack of 52 cards. Choose the dealer by someone dealing cards face up; the first to get a jack becomes the dealer. The dealer shuffles, and the player to his right cuts.

Cards are dealt one at a time, from the dealer's left, until the pack is used up.

Play begins from the dealer's left. The first card to be played must be a seven. If you have no seven, you pass, and pay a chip to the pool.

When a seven is put down, the six and eight of the same suit are also available for play, and once these are down, the next values above and below can be played.

The four sevens are laid in a row in the centre of the table, with the sixes to one side and the eights to the other. Suits can then be built up to the king and down to the ace, which is low.

Only one card can be played in each turn. If you can play a card, you must. If you pass when able to play, pay a penalty of three chips to the pool.

The first player to lay down all his cards wins. Others pay one chip for each card they are left holding, and the winner then takes the whole pool.

HELPFUL HINT: It's almost always best to play from your 'long suit' – the suit you have most cards in.

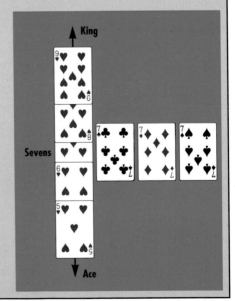

18

Cheat

AIM OF THE GAME: To be first to get rid of all the cards in your hand.

NUMBER OF PLAYERS: Three or more.

HOW TO PLAY: Use the 52-pack. Cut for dealer (higest card wins). The dealer deals all the cards, one at a time.

The player to the dealer's left leads, by placing face down one or more cards. He says what the cards are – but he may be lying about the number of cards, their suit and their value.

An opposing player may call 'Cheat!' at any point. The last player has then to turn his discards face up. If he was cheating, he has to pick up all the cards in the discard pile. If he was not cheating, the caller must take all the discards.

If there is no call, the next player to the left takes his turn, placing his cards face down on the cards already played. He can play only cards of the same value as those just announced, or the next rank up (ace if it was a king, two if it was an ace). But he may cheat.

HELPFUL HINTS: This can be an uproarious game. But watch the other players' faces – and try to keep your own deadpan. When you say what cards you are leading, look sneaky when telling the truth, and sincere when cheating – or the other way about.

Always challenge a player who is going out – you have nothing to lose.

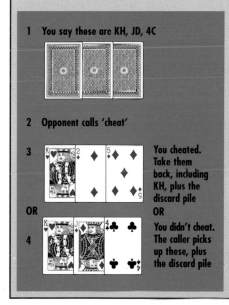

1 You say these are KH, JD, 4C

2 Opponent calls 'cheat'

3 You cheated. Take them back, including KH, plus the discard pile

OR

4 You didn't cheat. The caller picks up these, plus the discard pile

Hearts

AIM OF THE GAME: To win tricks without winning any cards from the hearts suit.

NUMBER OF PLAYERS: From three to six.

HOW TO PLAY: Use the standard pack of 52, but with three players, take out the two of clubs. This equalizes the hands. Cut for dealer (lowest card). Dealing goes to the left. All cards should be dealt out, one at a time.

The opening lead is made by the player on the dealer's left. Other players must follow suit if they can, otherwise any card may be played. There are no trumps. The highest card of the leading suit wins. The winning player leads to the next trick.

SCORING: The aim is to avoid collecting hearts and to lose any that one is dealt. Each time a player takes a heart, he loses a point.
At the end of the round, each player adds his score of hearts, adding one for each heart card he has. The lowest score wins the round. The game continues until one player reaches a score of 30. The player with the lowest score is the winner.

It's your lead   Your hand

Who shuffled this lot? Keep your hearts in the hope that you can lose them when you can't follow suit.
Play your KS or QC, and hope you won't pick up any more hearts

VARIANT 1: When three are playing, add the joker to the pack and subtract the two of clubs and two of diamonds, allowing each player to receive 17 cards. The joker makes an additional heart between the ten and the jack.

VARIANT 2: The queen of spades is an additional heart, but she scores 20 points if won. The ace of hearts scores 15, the court hearts score 10, and the other hearts score their pip value. Additionally, the heart cards are all trumps, although the queen of spades is not. In this version, the worst possible score in a hand is 120.

In this version, the game ends when someone reaches a total point score of 500. The player with the lowest score wins.

VARIANT 3: You can add further to the excitement by introducing a bonus card into the game. This is usually the jack of diamonds, and he counts for 20 plus-points, offsetting 'Black Maria', the queen of spades.

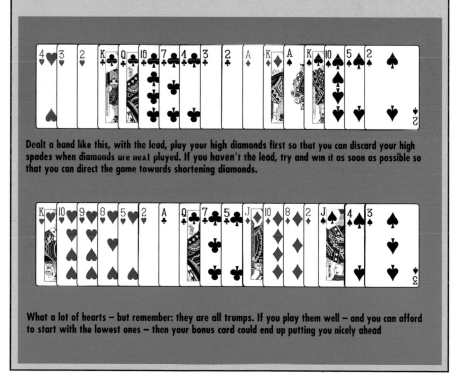

Dealt a hand like this, with the lead, play your high diamonds first so that you can discard your high spades when diamonds are next played. If you haven't the lead, try and win it as soon as possible so that you can direct the game towards shortening diamonds.

What a lot of hearts – but remember: they are all trumps. If you play them well – and you can afford to start with the lowest ones – then your bonus card could end up putting you nicely ahead

Five Hundred

AIM OF THE GAME: To make, or beat, the contract; and be first to score 500 points.

NUMBER OF PLAYERS: Two to six, but three is the ideal number.

HOW TO PLAY: Use a pack of 32 cards (standard pack excluding all cards between two and six inclusive), plus a joker. Draw for first deal: lowest card wins (ace low, joker lowest).

Deal to the left, ten cards to each player in packets of three-four-three. After the first round of three, three cards are laid face down in the centre. This is the widow. Having seen their hands, each player may make a single bid, or pass. Each bid states the number of tricks the player will take, from six to ten, and his trump suit (or no trumps), e.g. 'eight diamonds'; 'ten no trumps'. Each bid must be for a higher number of tricks than the bid before, or the same number if ten. The highest bid, or first to bid ten, becomes the contract.

If no one makes a bid, the dealt cards are collected, shuffled and redealt by the next dealer (player to the dealer's left). Bidding then resumes.

The other two players combine in alliance to defeat the bidder, but they may not see each other's hands.

The bidder takes up the widow, then discards any three cards from his hand. He can lead with any card. The others must follow suit, if able; if unable, any card may be played. The trick is won by the highest trump, or highest card of the suit led. The

winner of the trick leads to the next trick.

If the bidder had called no trumps, then the only trump is the joker. The trick can only be won by the highest card of the suit led, unless the joker is played, when it wins.

If a player leads with the joker, he must declare the suit that the others must follow, if they can.

TRUMPS: The ranking of suits, high to low, is: hearts, diamonds, clubs, spades. But a no trump bid outranks them all.

Card ranking in the trump suit: joker; jack; jack of the other suit of the same colour; ace; king; queen; ten; nine; eight; seven. Card ranking in the non-trump suits: ace, king, queen, jack (but see above); ten; nine; eight; seven.

SCORING: Each player keeps a running total from round to round. The bidder's opponents keep their scores separately. See the table for the number of points awarded.

If the bidder makes his contract,

he scores the value of his bid. If his bid added up to less than 250, and he actually takes all ten tricks, he is awarded only 250. If he is set back (fails to make his contract), then the value of his bid is subtracted from his running total. This can produce a minus figure. Each opponent scores ten points for every trick he wins.

Game is made at 500. If another player goes out (hits 500) on the same deal as the bidder, the bidder wins.

VARIANT: A player may bid 'nullo'. This is an offer to win no tricks, at no trump. Its scoring value is 250, so its bid value is between eight clubs and eight spades. If the nullo bidder gains the contract, he loses if he wins a single trick. Each of his opponents gains ten points for each trick made by the bidder.

NUMBER OF TRICKS BID

	6	7	8	9	10
No trump	120	220	320	420	520
Hearts	100	200	300	400	500
Diamonds	80	180	280	380	480
Clubs	60	160	260	360	460
Spades	40	140	240	340	440

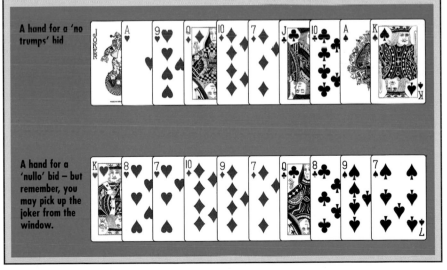

A hand for a 'no trumps' bid

A hand for a 'nullo' bid – but remember, you may pick up the joker from the window.

Nap

The full name is 'Napoleon', and it is a gambling game, a member of the Euchre game group.

AIM OF THE GAME: As highest bidder, to win the contracted number of tricks.

NUMBER OF PLAYERS: From two to six, but four makes the best game.

HOW TO PLAY: Use the standard pack of 52 cards. Aces are high, except when drawing for the deal, when they are low. Lowest card is first to deal and has choice of seat, with second lowest on his left, and so on.

Players pay an agreed number of tokens or coins into the pool. The dealer deals out five cards, one at a time, to each player, starting on his left.

On receipt of the cards, each player, starting on the dealer's left, must make a bid for the number of tricks that he will win, if he can name the trump suit. Each must either bid higher than the previous bid, or pass. If all pass, the dealer must make the minimal bid of at least one trick. Otherwise the lowest acceptable bid is two. To bid for all five tricks is to go nap.

The highest bidder makes the opening lead, and the suit he leads becomes trumps. Others must follow suit if they can, or play a discard. The highest trump, or highest card of the leading suit in the next trick, wins. The winner leads to the next trick.

The other players set out to play against the highest bidder. If the highest bidder wins tricks over and above his bid, he receives no credit. As soon as he has won

his forecast number of tricks, he must show his remaining cards to prove that he has not revoked at any point.

SCORING: If nap is made, it is worth ten points to the winner. If, having bid nap, the player fails to make it, he pays five points to the other players. If the player makes his bid, but it is less than nap, it is worth as many points as there are tricks; if he is defeated, he pays the same number of points to each of his opponents. Deals are settled at the end of each round.

HELPFUL HINTS: With only a part of the pack in play, the opportunities for bidding will be restricted, unless a very lucky hand is dealt. Even four assorted trumps, if they are not court cards, are only likely to win three tricks.

VARIANTS: Bidding can be increased if players are allowed to bid a Wellington. This is a bid to go nap, but doubles all the stakes. A player can only do this if nap has already been bid.

BIDDING MISERE. This is a bid that exceeds a bid for three tricks, but is itself exceeded by a bid for four. It offers an opportunity to a player with a poor hand, as it is a bid to take no tricks, on the basis of having no trumps.

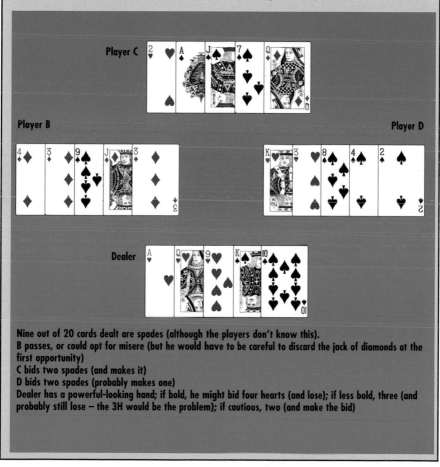

Nine out of 20 cards dealt are spades (although the players don't know this).
B passes, or could opt for misere (but he would have to be careful to discard the jack of diamonds at the first opportunity)
C bids two spades (and makes it)
D bids two spades (probably makes one)
Dealer has a powerful-looking hand; if bold, he might bid four hearts (and lose); if less bold, three (and probably still lose – the 3H would be the problem); if cautious, two (and make the bid)

Whist

This is one of the oldest card games, played for more than four hundred years. Familiarity with Whist makes a good introduction to the more complex game of Bridge, also played by two sets of partners.

AIM OF THE GAME: To take more tricks than the opposing partnership.

NUMBER OF PLAYERS: Four, playing as two sets of partners.

HOW TO PLAY: Use the pack of 52 cards. Normally two packs are employed, with different back designs or colours, so that one may be shuffled while the other is being dealt. Aces are high.

Players draw cards to decide partners, who sit facing each other across the table. The draw can be for the same suit or value. A draw is also made to find the dealer – highest card, with aces low.

The dealer deals out 13 cards to each player, one at a time, starting with the player to his left. The last card is turned face up to determine trumps: the dealer then adds it to his hand.

The player to the dealer's left leads. Others must follow suit if they can, otherwise trump or discard. The highest card of the led suit or a trump card wins. One partner from each side takes charge of the side's won tricks. The winner of a trick leads to the next trick.

SCORING: A partnership, or pair, has to take at least seven tricks to score. The first six tricks won have no scoring value. After the seventh, each trick counts for one point. Revoking is penalized by three points. The first side to gain five points wins the game. Points are also given for honour cards held. If a pair receive ace, king, queen and jack of the trump suit, they gain an extra four points. If they receive any three of the honour cards, they gain an extra two points. Points for honour cards are only given to a side which starts the deal with a score of less than four points.

Whist is normally played in a set of three games (a Rubber).

HELPFUL HINT: Unlike the other games in this book, Whist requires two partners to play together. They cannot show their hands to each other, nor give any information. Because of the follow-suit rule, opportunities for strategic play are fairly limited. But you need to watch your partner's lead very carefully. The normal lead is the fourth card in your longest suit. If you are not leading to make the trick, play low, to give your partner the chance to win it. This is the best way to conserve your high value cards for winning later tricks.

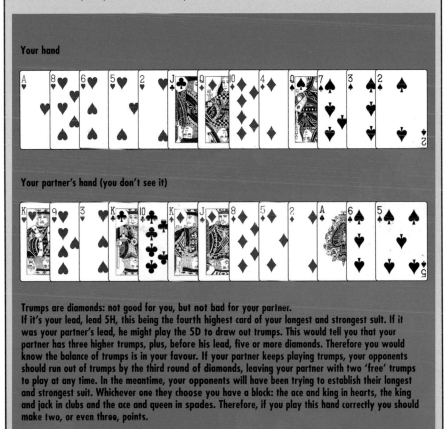

Your hand

Your partner's hand (you don't see it)

Trumps are diamonds: not good for you, but not bad for your partner.
If it's your lead, lead 5H, this being the fourth highest card of your longest and strongest suit. If it was your partner's lead, he might play the 5D to draw out trumps. This would tell you that your partner has three higher trumps, plus, before his lead, five or more diamonds. Therefore you would know the balance of trumps is in your favour. If your partner keeps playing trumps, your opponents should run out of trumps by the third round of diamonds, leaving your partner with two 'free' trumps to play at any time. In the meantime, your opponents will have been trying to establish their longest and strongest suit. Whichever one they choose you have a block: the ace and king in hearts, the king and jack in clubs and the ace and queen in spades. Therefore, if you play this hand correctly you should make two, or even three, points.

27

Pontoon

Known in the USA as 'Blackjack', and in France as 'Vingt-et-Un' (Twenty-One), this is one of the best-known of gambling games. You will need to provide tokens or cash for betting.

AIM OF THE GAME: To form a hand whose total value is 21, or which beats the dealer's.

NUMBER OF PLAYERS: From two to eight or more, but five to eight is best.

CARD VALUES: Ace can count as one or 11 at the players' choice; kings, queens, jacks and tens all count as ten; other cards follow their pip value.

HOW TO PLAY: Use the 52-card pack (two packs shuffled together for more than eight). Cut for banker (highest card; he is also the dealer).

The banker deals one card to each player, going from his left and ending with himself. His card remains face down; everyone else picks up their card. Again from the banker's left, the players place their initial bets (between agreed maximum and minimum levels). The banker deals a second card face down to each player, and now all the players, including the banker, look at their two cards. If the banker has a Pontoon (ace – at 11 – plus a card scoring ten), he lays it down, face up. Each player has to pay double their stake to the banker, and the round ends. If the banker cannot declare a Pontoon, then each player from his left has a turn to improve their hand by acquiring extra cards. A player with a Pontoon declares it by placing it on the table, the ten face down and the ace face up on top of it. A player with two cards of equal value can split, by laying them face up on the table

and placing another stake equal to his first one. The banker deals another card, face down, to each of these. If again there are equal-value cards, there can be a further split. Each of these hands may then be played, one after the other, during the player's turn.

Note: if the cards are ten-point ones, they must be of the same nominal rank; two jacks may be split, but a jack and a king cannot.

If a player's cards total under 21, he can say 'I'll buy one'. He must bet again by the same amount as before, or up to double it. The banker then deals him another card face down. If the total is still under 21, he can buy again, once more increasing his stake. This time, any amount between the first bet and the second. If the total is still under 21, he can buy and bet again, in the same way. Instead of buying, if his total is under 21, a player can say 'Twist'. This means no increase in the stake, and the banker deals him another card face down. The player can then Twist again if his total is low, until he has up to five cards in his hand. Five cards totalling under 21 form a Five Card Trick. A player can buy and then twist, but not twist and then buy.

A player may decide to take no extra cards, and say 'Stick'. This is usual if his hand totals 15 or more. Play then passes to the next player on the left.

If at any time a player's hand exceeds 21, he is 'bust', and must throw in his hand, face up, and lose his stake to the bank. A player who is bust on one split hand can still play the other.

When the players have completed their turns, the banker turns his two cards face up. He can then add up to three extra cards, or stay with his hand.

At the end of the round, after scoring is completed, there are several possibilities: If no one had a Pontoon, the dealer adds all the used cards to the bottom of the pack and deals again, without shuffling. If there was a Pontoon, the cards are shuffled and cut before the next deal. The banker does not change unless he did not have a Pontoon, and another player did have one, without splitting his hand. That player takes over the bank. If two or more players are eligible, then the one nearest the banker's left becomes the new banker. A banker can also sell the bank to another player, after any round.

SCORING: If the banker has over 21, he is bust. He pays their stakes back to all players who have not also gone bust, with double to anyone with a Pontoon or a Five Card Trick. If the banker has 21 or less, with not more than four cards, he pays their stake back to any player with a higher hand value, and collects from those with an equal or lower value. A banker who stayed on 19 will say 'Paying 20'. All players then show their cards; those with 21 or a Five Card Trick receive double their stake. A banker with 21 pays only Pontoons and Five Card Tricks. If the banker has a Five Card Trick, he pays only Pontoons (double the stake). Every other player, even those with Five Card Tricks, pay double their stake to the banker.

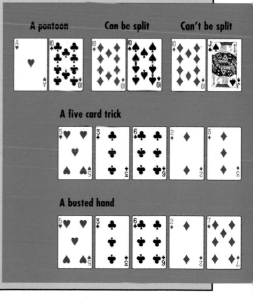

A pontoon   Can be split   Can't be split

A five card trick

A busted hand

Poker

There are many different sorts of poker, but this one (Five-Draw Poker) shows the essential game.

AIM OF THE GAME: To have the highest-ranking hand at the end of the game.

NUMBER OF PLAYERS: Four or more.

HOW TO PLAY: Use the 52-card pack. Aces are high. The suits are all of equal value. The dealer is chosen by anyone dealing from a shuffled pack: first to get a jack becomes the first dealer. The cards are shuffled three times, lastly by the dealer, and the player to dealer's right cuts. Cards are dealt one at a time, from the dealer's left, until each player has five cards.

BETTING: Stakes should be agreed in advance (cash or chips). Each player antes a chip into the pool at the start. One player acts as Banker. Betting normally starts to the dealer's left and goes clockwise.

You can either call, raise or fold (sometimes called drop). If you fold, you discard your hand and lose your stake. If you call, you must put into the pool enough chips to match, but not exceed, what any other player has bet in that round. If you raise, you add more value to the call amount, subject to an agreed upper limit.

When you raise, you must say clearly the amount you are raising by.

Once everyone has made a bet, or folded, the remaining players discard up to three cards, and receive replacement cards from the dealer. Another betting round follows and you can again call, raise or fold. Previous bets cannot be withdrawn. At the end of each betting round, each player has to have put the same amount into the pool. If you don't do this, you have to fold.

Then hands are shown (the showdown). The highest hand wins the pot.

HELPFUL HINTS: Poker is a mix of luck and psychology. You have to watch your fellow players closely, and study their bets. If you hold a high hand, don't look too pleased or others will not raise the stakes and you will win less. If you have a low-scoring hand, fold unless you are feeling particularly lucky. If another player discards only one card, it's a danger signal – or a bluff. After all, this is the game that gave rise to the expression 'poker-face'.

SCORING

Poker hands consist of five cards. Each type of hand has a rank relative to the others – below is a list from highest ranked to lowest:

STRAIGHT FLUSH: Five cards in suit and sequence, ace being either high or low. A Royal Flush (ace-high straight flush) beats any other.

FOUR OF A KIND: Four cards of the same value (e.g. four kings or four twos), plus any other card.

FULL HOUSE: Three of one kind and a pair of another kind (e.g. three kings and two twos).

FLUSH: Five cards all of the same suit, but not in sequence.

STRAIGHT: Five cards in complete sequence of rank, ace either high or low, but of different suits.

THREE OF A KIND: Three cards of the same value, plus two others which are not a pair.

TWO PAIRS: Two sets of two of the same value, plus any other card.

PAIR: One set of two of the same value, plus any three other cards

HIGH CARD: Any hand which is not one of those listed above. If nobody has a Pair or better, then the highest card wins. If there is a tie for highest, then the next highest card wins.

Sample combinations

	Five of a Kind
	Royal Flush
	Straight Flush
	Full House
	Flush
	Three of a Kind
	Two Pairs
	High Card

VARIANT: Once you have mastered Five-Draw Poker, you can introduce Wild Cards, either by using a joker in the pack, or by naming another card as wild. With a joker, you can make a hand called Five of a Kind, which beats a Royal Flush (five aces is top, then five kings, etc.).

Knaves

AIM OF THE GAME: To win the greatest number of tricks, without taking any jacks (knaves).

HOW TO PLAY: Use the 52-card pack. Cut for dealer (highest card). The dealer deals 17 cards to each player, one card at a time. The remaining card is turned over to denote trumps for the round.

The player to the dealer's left leads by laying down a card. Other players must follow suit, trump, or discard a card. Continue until all cards are played.

SCORING: Each trick won receives one point. The first player to reach 20 points wins the game. But any trick containing a jack is penalized by deducting points as follows: jack of hearts, four; diamonds, three; clubs, two; spades, one.

HELPFUL HINT: If you hold a jack, don't lead with it, or your opponents may force you to win the trick, and so lose points.

REVOKING: This is failing to follow suit in a trick when you are able to. If you correct the error before the trick is turned over, there is no penalty. If you are caught – although only before the start of the next trick – you cannot win the trick, and you incur a three-point penalty.

Penalty points for jacks

CARD TRICKS

INTRODUCTION

♦♣♥♠♦♣♥♠♦♣♥♠♦♣

All the tricks in this book are easy to learn and simple to perform.
Even so, a little time spent in rehearsal will enhance their impact
and improve your reputation as a performer.

So how much practice does a card trick need? Enough to ensure
you perform it smoothly and can handle the cards with confidence.
No one believes in a performer who is nervous, or who is
not in control of the material. Practise until a trick becomes
second nature, and you will give your presentation the
polish these fine tricks deserve.

It is also a good idea to memorize the two golden rules of magical
performance. Rule One: Never do the same trick twice for the
same audience, no matter how hard they plead with you.
Rule Two: Never bore your audience. Stop performing while
they are still keen to see more. That way, you will be asked to
entertain them another time.

Above all else, enjoy your magic. Card tricks are designed to
divert and entertain, and there is no reason why you shouldn't
enjoy each performance as much as your audience does.

CHATTY JOKER

THE METHOD

You need two identical Jokers. Cut one in half and write your message on the other. Put the Joker with the message face up on top of the pack. Put the half Joker over it and hold them together with an elastic band around the middle (Fig. 1); thus the half Joker will be held in place and its missing bottom concealed. On the face of it, the top card is a complete Joker.

❖❖❖❖❖❖❖❖❖❖❖

To perform, drop the pack of cards on the table, drawing attention to the Joker: 'That's a very clever card,' you say. 'It can always get its message across.'

1

Pick up the cards and start to pull out the Joker from under the elastic band, grasping it at the lower end – that is, you are taking out the complete Joker. As you do so, turn the packet over so that it is face down by the time you draw the Joker out. Put the Joker face down on the table. Drop the cards into your pocket. In the same move, take out your pen and lay it a short distance from the card. Tell a spectator to put one hand on the pen and the other on the card. 'Now,' you say, 'close your eyes and count to three.' Then tell the spectator to turn the card. The message will be there for all to see.

TURN-OVER CARD MYSTERY

THE EFFECT

A spectator takes a card from the pack and remembers it. It is put back, and when the pack is spread, the chosen card has turned face up.

THE METHOD

Before you begin, turn the bottom card of the face-down pack face up. When you spread the cards (Fig. 1), make sure the bottom card doesn't show.

❖❖❖❖❖❖❖❖❖❖❖

1

Ask the spectator to take a card, then square the pack in your left hand and tell him or her to let others see it. 'Tonight, I'll allow witnesses,' you say.

As the card is shown around, your left hand drops casually to your side; on the way down, let the pack turn over in your hand. Do not rush this.

When you bring the hand up again, you are holding a squared-up pack with one face-down card on top. The rest are face up.

2

sight for only a moment, and everyone believes it was just a swift gag.

'But I'm a first-rate operator,' you say, 'so I use real magic.' Put the pack face-down on the table, and prepare to spread the cards in a long ribbon. 'What was the name of your card?' you ask. As soon as the card is named, spread the

Take the chosen card from the spectator, keeping it face down, and push it very deliberately into the pack **(Fig. 2)**. Square up the cards.

'If I were a beginner at this,' you say, 'I'd try to find your card like this...'

Put the pack behind your back and look worried, like someone hopelessly fumbling for a card. In fact, you turn the top card over to face the same way as the rest, then turn over the whole pack, so it is face down. Bring the cards into view. They have been out of

3

pack **(Fig. 3)**, and reveal the chosen card, now amazingly face upwards in the spread.

CARD SHARP

THE EFFECT

You mix the cards to a spectator's instructions, but they end up the same as they were at the start. The first time you do this trick it will probably fool you, too!

THE METHOD

Take all thirteen cards of one suit and lay them in numerical order on the table (Fig. 1). Tell a spectator to note the strict order of the cards, then square up the pile and turn it face down in your left hand.

❖❖❖❖❖❖❖❖❖❖

'We want to make sure the cards are thoroughly mixed,' you say, 'so you will tell me how to deal them.'

Explain that when the spectator says 'Deal', you will put a card on the table **(Fig. 2)**. When he or she says 'Dip', you will take the second card from the pile and put it on top of the first card **(Fig. 3)**, then deal both cards together on to the table.

You proceed to deal all the cards into a pile on the table, following the spectator's instructions to

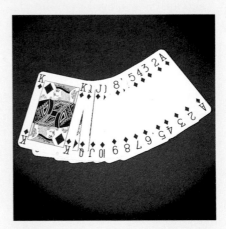

1

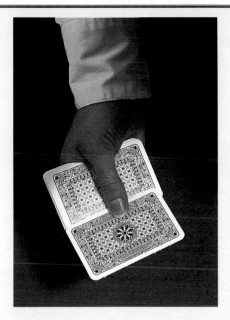

2

'Deal' or 'Dip' until all the cards are dealt. Now pick up the pile and square it.

'That has upset the order of the cards,' you say, 'but to upset them even further, we will go through the procedure once again.'

Once more you deal out the cards, carefully 'Dealing' or 'Dipping' as

instructed. When all are dealt, pick up the pile and say:

'The truth is, whatever you tell me to do, the cards always go where I tell them to go.'

Turn over the cards and spread them in a line.

3

Sure enough, all thirteen are back in numerical order, just as they were at the start.

THE ESTIMATE

THE EFFECT

You obtain an estimate of a card's position in the pack. The estimate seems unlikely, but it turns out to be right.

THE METHOD

Tear a quarter off a card. Place the card under five face-down cards (Fig. 1). Mark the upper left corner of the top card. Conceal the cards at the bottom of the pack.

❖❖❖❖❖❖❖❖❖❖

1

Say, 'Remember your card, then put it face down on top of the pack.' The spectator complies. 'Now give the pack a complete cut, burying your card.' The

To perform, spread the pack, being careful to keep the bottom cards bunched together to conceal the torn card. Ask a spectator to take a card **(Fig. 2)**. When he or she has done that, put the pack on the table.

2

3

Put the card to your ear. Listen and nod slowly. Put the card on the bottom of the pack and say, 'The estimate is four and three-quarters.'

Count the cards aloud, from the top of the pack. As you say, 'Four,' put down the fourth card and lift the mutilated one. **(Fig. 4)** '...And, er, three-quarters '

chosen card will now be directly under the torn card.

'I'm going to find your card by detecting its vibrations,' you announce, and begin to thumb through the face-down cards. When you see the card with the dot, cut it to the top so that the card and the cards beneath it move to the top **(Fig. 3)**. Then square the pack. Look confident as you turn over the marked card and say, 'Is this your card?' It isn't. You sigh and say you knew all along this wasn't the card: 'I just chose this one because it'll give me an estimate...'

4

Drop the torn card and pick up the next one. Ask the spectator to name the chosen card. Turn over the card in your hand and reveal that your earlier estimate was correct.

EDUCATED CARDS

THE EFFECT

You take turns with a spectator at laying cards on the table. You put down a card which bears the prophetic message 'You've Run Out Of Cards'.

THE METHOD

Make the message card by sticking a label across the face of another card. (Fig. 1). Place this card at the twenty-first position from the top of the face-down pack.

❖❖❖❖❖❖❖❖❖❖❖

1

To perform, ask a spectator to cut some cards from the top of the pack, which is on the table, and put them in his or her pocket.

'Not too many,' you tell them, 'or we'll be here all night...' This ensures that fewer than twenty-one cards are taken! 'And now I'll have some.'

You must take twenty-one cards, and reverse their order. To do this, pick up the pack and deal twenty-one cards on to the table, one on top of the other **(Fig. 2)**; don't make it obvious that you are

42

2

3

counting. Put the pack aside and pick up your twenty-one cards.

'Right,' you say, 'now we'll deal cards on the table alternately. Me first.'

You deal a card, turning it face up as you do, then the spectator takes one from his or her pocket and deals it **(Fig. 3)**. Continue until you deal the message card. The spectator reaches in his or her pocket and finds that all the cards have gone **(Fig. 4)**.

As you'll discover, this trick is

entirely automatic, but it gives the impression of considerable skill on the part of the performer.

4

43

MENTAL GUIDANCE

THE EFFECT

A spectator picks a card. Without looking, he pushes another card into the pack right beside his selection. You locate the spectator's selection. How?

THE METHOD

Tell the spectator to take half the pack, give you the rest and put their half behind their back. He or she takes out any card, looks at it, then puts it on top of their pack.

❖❖❖❖❖❖❖❖❖❖

'I'll show you first,' you say. Put your half behind your back; turn the second card face-upwards **(Fig. 1)**. Do this by lifting two cards with the right hand, pulling

2

1

the second card down with with the left thumb and flipping it over before the other card is dropped on top. This takes less than a

3

this: push the top card into the pack near the bottom; push the bottom card in near the top; then turn the top card face up and push it in anywhere near the centre **(Fig. 3)**. 'As you push this one in,' you say, 'I will send you mental guidance.'

NOTE: The insertion of top and bottom cards is a red herring. It gets the spectator accustomed to the manoeuvre – and it brings the turned-over card to the top!

second and should happen as the cards are being put behind your back. Now slip off the bottom card and bring it into view **(Fig. 2)**, to demonstrate that you have chosen a card. Put the card behind you again, but put it *face up* on the bottom of your pack, which you bring to the front.

'Now do as I showed you,' you say. When this has been done, the spectator brings his or her cards to the front and you put yours on top. 'Now your card is buried,' you say.

Tell the spectator to put the whole pack behind them and do

The big finish. Spread the cards, showing there is one face-up near the centre, as expected **(Fig. 4)**. But beneath it is the card chosen by the spectator, located through your mental guidance.

4

ASTOUNDING!

THE EFFECT

You predict the identity of a card freely-chosen under seemingly impossible conditions.

THE METHOD

Any Ace and any Four must be removed from the pack and set aside. Do this openly, keeping the cards face down, explaining that they are your prediction cards.

❖❖❖❖❖❖❖❖❖❖

To perform, hand the pack to a spectator to shuffle, and ask him or her to think of a number between one and ten, which they must keep to themselves. Now tell the spectator to put the pack under the table and remove the number of cards that corresponds to their chosen number – i.e., if their number is four, they remove four cards **(Fig. 1)**. The spectator must put those cards in his pocket and hand back the pack.

'Now I'm going to start counting the pack,' you say, 'and when I get to the number you're thinking of, I want you to memorize it.' You

1

count the cards off the top of the pack, calling the number of each as you show its face, reversing the

46

2

never questioned. You have dealt thirteen cards in total. Put the dealt cards on top of the pack, and almost as an after-thought hold out the pack and tell the spectator to put back the cards they took off **(Fig. 3)**. The spectator's chosen card is fourteenth from the top. This is automatic. Show the Ace and Four you removed at the start.

order as you put them down **(Fig. 2)**.

Count this way until you reach number ten; count one more, saying 'Eleven', then ask if the spectator has remembered his or her card. As you say this, show and deal two more cards, without calling out numbers. This action is

4

'Fourteen,' you say. 'That is my prediction.'

Tell the spectator to count down to the fourteenth card **(Fig. 4)** and put it on the table, face down. When that is done, ask for the name of his card. Pause, then turn over the card on the table. Astounding!

3

PRECOGNITION

THE EFFECT

Put a sealed envelope containing your precognition on the table. A spectator chooses a card, and is asked to open the envelope. Inside is a duplicate of their chosen card.

THE METHOD

To prepare, put a duplicate of the 'force' card (here the Eight of Hearts) in an envelope. The Eight of Hearts in your pack should be the tenth card from the top of the pack.

❖❖❖❖❖❖❖❖❖❖

To perform, tell a spectator that you will persuade him or her to choose a card according to the laws of numerology, but that the numbers will be of his or her own choosing. Hand over the pack and ask for a number between ten and twenty. (The trick won't work with twenty!) Let's assume they pick sixteen. Tell them to deal sixteen cards on to the table.

'Now put the rest of the pack aside and add together the digits of your chosen number,' you say. The number was sixteen; 1 + 6 = 7. Tell the spectator to pick up the

1

sixteen cards and count down to the seventh. This card should be turned face up **(Fig. 1)**. The card in the envelope will be identical to the one chosen by the spectator.

GROUP REVELATION

THE EFFECT

Freely chosen cards are distributed among spectators. One by one, you reveal each of their selections.

THE METHOD

The stacked pack is spread face down as you approach a spectator. 'Pull out a bunch of cards,' you say. 'Keep one for yourself and hand out the rest to other spectators.'

❖❖❖❖❖❖❖❖❖❖

When the cards have been removed, cut the pack at that point, putting the lower part on top. Square the cards, glimpsing the bottom card. Let's say the spectator took six cards, and the card you glimpsed was the King of Diamonds (**Fig. 1**). Now pretend you are gaining an impression of a dark card. Of course you start with the card which would have followed the King of Diamonds – the Three of Clubs. Name the card and ask if anyone has it. When it is returned, put it at the bottom of the pack. Do the same with each successive card you reveal.

1

As you proceed with the revelations, you will find that people react in a way that shows you are about to name their card. Use these clues to home in on individuals. This will reinforce the idea that you're receiving 'spirit' messages!

THE BUCKLE

THE EFFECT

You find a selected card while holding the pack behind your back.

THE METHOD

Spread out the pack, face down, and ask for a card to be chosen. As the spectator looks at the card, close the pack and buckle it upwards (Fig. 1).

❖❖❖❖❖❖❖❖❖❖

1

Spread the cards again and let the spectator put back his or her card anywhere they like. Hand the

pack to the spectator for shuffling.

The chosen card is now the only flat card, which means the pack is markedly divided at the place where the card is inserted; the card automatically becomes the key **(Fig. 2)**.

Take back the cards and square them. You will be able to see the break. If the chosen card is close to the top or bottom of the pack, make a cut to put it nearer the centre. If the card is right on the top or bottom of the pack, leave it where it is.

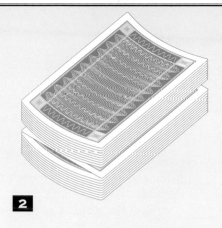

Put the cards behind your back, saying you will find the selected card by feeling its emanations.

With the pack behind your back, hold the cards lightly with the right thumb on one long edge and the right fingers on the other **(Fig 3)**. Now gently cut the cards and you will feel them break naturally. The chosen card, which is now wider than the others, will be the bottom card of the upper part of the cut. Slide it out into your right hand **(Fig. 4)** and put the rest of the cards in your left hand.

Smile as you bring out the pack and put it down.

Widen your smile as you bring forward the chosen card and put it face up on the table.

3

4

MOVING FINGER

THE EFFECT

A spectator makes you find his card – even though he has no idea where it is.

THE METHOD

Your key is the top card of the pack. It is not gimmicked, but on its back you have marked diagonally opposite corners with a pencil dot (Fig. 1).

❖❖❖❖❖❖❖❖❖❖

1

Ask for a card to be selected, then cut the pack with your right hand. Offer the lower half for the return of the card.

The cards in your right hand are turned over ready for an overhand shuffle and the key card (top) is drawn on to the lower pile **(Figs. 2 and 3)**. Continue to shuffle the other cards on top. This looks perfectly fair, but of course the key card is now on top of the chosen card. When you have shuffled off all the cards, give the pack a couple of cuts then spread it face down in a ribbon across the table, noting the position of the key card.

2

Begin above one end of the ribbon and let the spectator draw your hand slowly along. You know the card with the dot (the key) is on the right of the chosen card. When you are almost above the key, start to bring your hand down. To the audience, your hand is being guided.

Let your finger come to rest on the card to the left of the key. Slide it out with your fingertips.

'Name your card,' you say.

The spectator names it. Turn over the card. You have performed a miracle.

3

4

Ask the spectator to hold your wrist, then extend your arm over the cards at a height of about 50 cm (20 in), your finger pointing down **(Fig. 4).**

'You don't know where your card is,' you say. 'Neither do I. But concentrate on its name.'

BLINDFOLD MIND PROBE

THE EFFECT

You are blindfolded. A card is selected as usual. Without asking any questions, you correctly name the card.

THE METHOD

Arrange the cards so they run in the order Ace, 4, 7, 10, King, 3, 6, 9, Queen, 2, 5, 8, Jack, and in the repeating order of Clubs, Hearts, Spades, Diamonds (Fig. 1).

❖❖❖❖❖❖❖❖❖❖❖

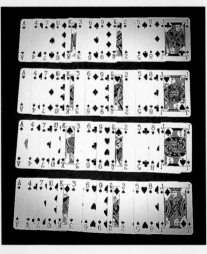

1

Each card is three higher than the one before – e.g., if you cut a Two, the card beneath it will be a Five; cut a Nine and the next card will be twelve (a Queen). The suit order – Clubs, Hearts, Spades, Diamonds – is remembered by picturing the word CHaSeD. If you cut the Three of Hearts, the next card is the Six of Spades.

To perform the trick blindfold, have the stacked pack ready in your hands; it can be cut as often as you wish without disturbing the stack. Ask a spectator to blindfold you with a large handkerchief, which you adjust 'for comfort', with your thumbs, so you can see clearly down either side of your nose.

Spread the cards face down between your hands and ask for one to be chosen **(Fig. 2)**. As it is taken, cut the pack at that point and put the bottom portion on top. Turn the pack face up for a moment as you square it and you will see the bottom card **(Fig. 3)** – let's say it's the Seven of Clubs.

3

Put down the cards. Ask the spectator to concentrate on his card.

The bottom card of the pack was originally above the selected card; it's a Seven, so the chosen card must be a Ten – and it is a Club, so the chosen card must be a Heart. The Ten of Hearts.

'I'm getting an impression,' you say, as soon as you have made the simple calculation. Slowly name the card.

2

THOUGHT PROCESS

THE EFFECT

The selections of two spectators are divined before they themselves know what cards they have chosen.

THE METHOD

You will need two stacked packs. Put one pack in front of one spectator, hand another spectator the second pack and tell him or her to put it behind their back.

❖❖❖❖❖❖❖❖❖❖

Address the first spectator. 'Cut that pack as many times as you want, complete cuts, putting the top half underneath each time.' When that is done, say, 'Take off the top card, don't look at it, and put it in your pocket. Now take the next card, no looking, and sit on it. Put the pack on the table.'

Turn to the second spectator. 'Cut the pack behind your back, then take off the top card, turn it face up, and slip it into the middle of the face-down pack.' **(Fig. 1)**

Turn to the first spectator again.

1

'I'm going to repeat your actions,' you say, 'and try to make my

2

thought process recover the image of what you did.'

Pick up the pack and glimpse the bottom card (e.g. the Five of Spades) **(Fig. 2)**. Now mime the action of taking a card from the top and pocketing it, then taking a second card and sitting on it.

'Now I'll look,' you say. Take the invisible card from your pocket and name it: 'The Eight of Diamonds' (the card after the Five of Spades). Ask the spectator to remove the card from his pocket. It matches!

Go through the same manoeuvre with the invisible card you sat on; stare at it, then say, 'the Jack of Clubs' (the card after the Eight of Diamonds). Ask the spectator to reveal his sat upon card. Again, a match! Turn to the second spectator and say, 'Put the pack face up on the table.'

He or she does this **(Fig. 3)**. You see which card is on top of the pack (e.g. the Ace of Clubs). You do a quick calculation, then announce, 'The card you reversed in the pack is the Four of Hearts.'

Spread the pack, find the face-down card, and turn it over – the Four of Hearts. You are a legend.

3

INTERLOPER

THE EFFECT

While you are out of the room, a card is freely chosen from the pack, then put back. You return, look through the cards and name the one that was chosen.

THE METHOD

The pack is stacked. Ask a spectator to cut it as many times as he or she likes. When this has been done, square it up and put it in the middle of the table.

❖❖❖❖❖❖❖❖❖❖

'I'm leaving the room,' you say. 'While I'm out, I want you to reach into the pack and take out a card. Show it to everyone, then put it back on top and cut it into the pack. When you've done that, call me in again.' When you return to the room, pick up the cards and turn them face up. Spread them between your hands **(Fig. 1)**, saying, 'In the last couple of minutes, one card of these fifty-two has suffered a little more disturbance than the others. I should be able to sense its stress as it passes through my fingers.'

The place where the card is inserted, however, will have a card which is out of sequence **(Fig. 3).** (In the picture the odd card is the Seven of Hearts.)

When you find the card, pull it out.

'I was right,' you say. 'This is a very badly stressed card.'

Turn it around and show its face. 'Poor thing.'

2

Start to go through the cards, taking your time. You note only the suits. The sequence of Clubs, Hearts, Spades, Diamonds is repeated over and over, all the way through the pack, except at the place where a card was removed, and at the place where it was replaced.

You will know where it was taken from, because there will simply be a gap in the sequence **(Fig. 2).**

3

CUTTING THE ACES

THE EFFECT

Magicians often demonstrate their skill by cutting the Aces; in this version, a spectator emulates this without knowing how it was done!

THE METHOD

A fresh pack of cards is prepared by putting the four Aces on top of the pack. The trick is to keep your eye on the pile with the four Aces on top.

❖❖❖❖❖❖❖❖❖❖❖

1

Put the cards on the table and ask a spectator to cut them into four roughly equal piles **(Fig. 1)**. Say, 'I want you to mix the top cards in the following way.' Point at a pile (not the one with the Aces), tell the spectator to pick it up, transfer three cards from the top to the bottom of the pile, then put one card on the top of each of the three piles on the table **(Fig. 2)**. The spectator must now put down

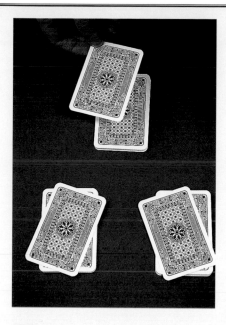

2

pile is picked up and the transferring is carried out for the last time. When the fourth pile is back on the table, ask if the spectator knows what has happened. The answer will probably be 'no'. 'Well,' you say, 'if my guess is correct, it's something pretty spectacular …' Turn over the top cards one by one **(Fig. 3)**, and show how clever spectators can be when they do as they're told.

3

the stack he or she is holding and repeat the actions with the other three piles. Point to the piles in turn, being careful to point last to the pile with the four Aces.

By the time the fourth pile is picked up, the procedure of transferring cards from other piles will have put three extra cards on top of the Aces. These will go to the bottom of the pile when the Ace

COUNTDOWN

THE EFFECT

Although the performer never touches the cards, he knows exactly where a chosen card lies in the pack.

THE METHOD

From bottom to top, stack the Ace to Ten of any one suit (e.g. Diamonds) (Fig. 1). The cards are in this position when you put the pack, face down, in front of a spectator.

❖❖❖❖❖❖❖❖❖❖

1

'From now on,' you say, 'I'm not going to touch the cards. I want you to spread the pack and slide out one card, then square up the pack again.'

Now tell the spectator to look at the card removed from the pack. 'Put it back on top and give the pack a full cut, which will bury the card.'

When the card is buried, tell the

2

3

spectator to turn the pack face up, rest a fingertip on the top card for a second **(Fig. 2)**, then give the pack another complete cut. What happens next will depend on how the pack is cut. As soon as the top card is a Diamond with a value anywhere between Ace and Ten, you know where the chosen card lies. For example, if the spectator cuts the Four of Diamonds to the top of the pack, then the chosen card will be at position number four when the pack is face down. If no Diamond card shows, ask the spectator to press a finger on the top card again (a red herring!) and cut once more. As soon as a Diamond

between Ace and Ten shows, remember it – let's say it's the Three **(Fig. 3)**. Tell the spectator to turn the pack face down. 'Put a finger on the pack again and think of your card,' you say. 'I sense its position.... It's at number five from the top. Whoops! You moved! Now it's at number four ... No, you moved again. Now it's at number three. Take a look. Quick, before it moves again!'

The spectator counts to number three (or whatever) and there, sure enough, is the chosen card **(Fig. 4)**.

4

INSTANT SPELL

THE EFFECT

A spectator finds his own chosen card by spelling its name. Of all the methods of achieving this classic effect, this is the most direct.

THE METHOD

Put the Ten of Clubs, Six of Spades, Jack of Hearts, Eight of Spades, and Nine and Queen of Diamonds face down on the pack, then nine assorted cards on top.

❖❖❖❖❖❖❖❖❖❖

To perform, start moving cards from the your left hand to your right, without reversing their order **(Fig. 1)**. As you reach the fifth or sixth card, say, 'Stop me when you like.' Speak a little impatiently – you will almost certainly be stopped on one of the set-up cards. (If you are not stopped on a set-up card, change tack; spot the bottom card of the pack and perform a 'key card' trick!)

Show the spectator the card he or she stopped at, and say, 'Look at this card and remember it.' Put the card back on the pack and drop all the right-hand cards on

top of it. The pack is now as it was at the start. Hand the cards to the spectator and ask them to spell the name of their card, starting from the top of the pack, including the word 'of'. The spectator's card will show up on the final letter 'S'.

1